Inka Terraces

Ben Nussbaum

✴ **Smithsonian**

Contributing Author

Allison Duarte

Consultants

Amy Van Allen, Ph.D.
Senior Project Manager
National Museum of the American Indian

Tanya Thrasher (Cherokee Nation)
Publications Manager and Editor-In-Chief
National Museum of the American Indian

Stephanie Anastasopoulos, M.Ed.
TOSA, STREAM Integration
Solana Beach School District

Publishing Credits

Rachelle Cracchiolo, M.S.Ed., *Publisher*
Conni Medina, M.A.Ed., *Managing Editor*
Diana Kenney, M.A.Ed., NBCT, *Content Director*
Véronique Bos, *Creative Director*
Robin Erickson, *Art Director*
Michelle Jovin, M.A., *Associate Editor*
Mindy Duits, *Senior Graphic Designer*
Smithsonian Science Education Center

Image Credits: p.8 Shiona Webster/Alamy; p.9 (top) Wendy White/Alamy; p.14 (insert) Library of Congress [LC-DIG-hec-15992]; p.19 Peter Horree/Alamy; p.23 McKay Savage; p.26 (insert) Cookie/Anna; pp.26–27 Laurent Giraudou/Sygma via Getty Images; all other images from iStock and/or Shutterstock.

Library of Congress Cataloging-in-Publication Data

Names: Nussbaum, Ben, 1975- author.
Title: Inka terraces / Ben Nussbaum.
Description: Huntington Beach, CA : Teacher Created Materials, Inc., [2019]
|
  Audience: Grade 4 to 6. | Includes index. |
Identifiers: LCCN 2018018110 (print) | LCCN 2018026656 (ebook) | ISBN
  9781493869503 (E-book) | ISBN 9781493867103 (paperback)
Subjects: LCSH: Incas--History--Juvenile literature. | Incas--Social life and
  customs--Juvenile literature. | Peru--Civilization--Juvenile literature. |
  Peru--Historical geography--Juvenile literature.
Classification: LCC F3429 (ebook) | LCC F3429 .N87 2019 (print) | DDC
  985/.019--dc23
LC record available at https://lccn.loc.gov/2018018110

Teacher Created Materials

5301 Oceanus Drive
Huntington Beach, CA 92649-1030
www.tcmpub.com
ISBN 978-1-4938-6710-3

Table of Contents

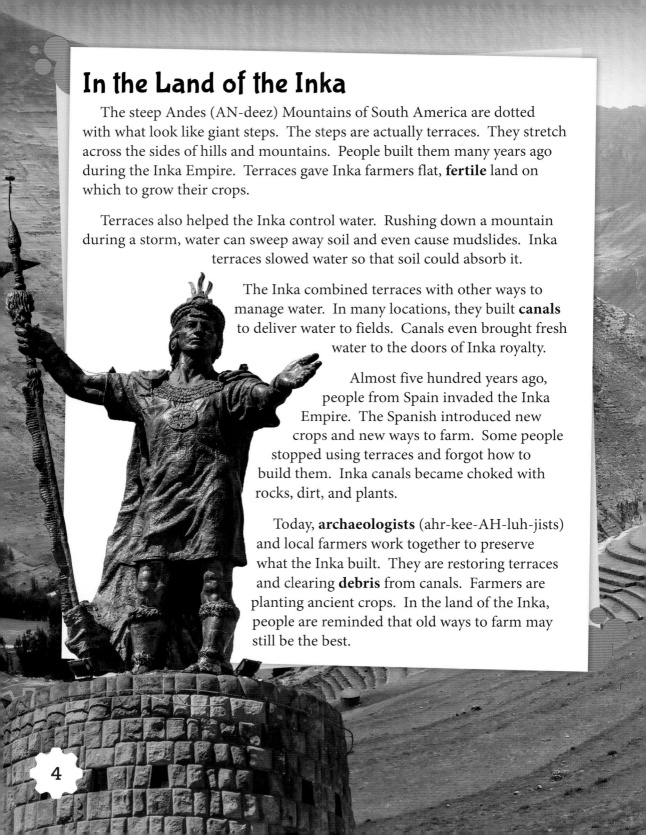

In the Land of the Inka

The steep Andes (AN-deez) Mountains of South America are dotted with what look like giant steps. The steps are actually terraces. They stretch across the sides of hills and mountains. People built them many years ago during the Inka Empire. Terraces gave Inka farmers flat, **fertile** land on which to grow their crops.

Terraces also helped the Inka control water. Rushing down a mountain during a storm, water can sweep away soil and even cause mudslides. Inka terraces slowed water so that soil could absorb it.

The Inka combined terraces with other ways to manage water. In many locations, they built **canals** to deliver water to fields. Canals even brought fresh water to the doors of Inka royalty.

Almost five hundred years ago, people from Spain invaded the Inka Empire. The Spanish introduced new crops and new ways to farm. Some people stopped using terraces and forgot how to build them. Inka canals became choked with rocks, dirt, and plants.

Today, **archaeologists** (ahr-kee-AH-luh-jists) and local farmers work together to preserve what the Inka built. They are restoring terraces and clearing **debris** from canals. Farmers are planting ancient crops. In the land of the Inka, people are reminded that old ways to farm may still be the best.

The Andes are the longest mountain chain in the world. They are almost three times as long as the Appalachian Mountains in the United States.

Terrific Terraces

Hills and mountains may be beautiful, but they aren't great for farming. One problem is that during heavy rain, water flows downhill instead of soaking into the soil. As a result, the bottom of the hill absorbs more water than the top of the hill. Another problem is **erosion**. Over time, the flow of water washes away the fertile soil that plants grow in. Rain water can also wash away seeds and destroy plants.

Terrace farming is a great solution. Today, people all over the world use terraces. In Asia, terraces planted with rice are common sights. In Europe, rows of grapes grow in terraced **vineyards**. In the United States, farmers drive tractors on wide terraces that are planted with wheat and soybeans. Many people use retaining walls in their yards. This is a simple kind of terrace.

The Inka did not invent terraces. They improved and combined techniques that already existed. Then, they spread their new ways to farm and build around the empire.

retaining walls in a front yard

terraced rice fields
in Yangshuo, China

In the Inka Empire, people did not pay money for taxes. Instead, they had to spend some time each year working for the state. This is how the Inka were able to create a vast number of terraces, as well as canals, roads, buildings, and other structures.

Terraces start with strong stone walls. The Inka pushed or carried each heavy stone to the right location, cut it with simple tools, and lifted it into place.

The Inka typically did not use mortar, the thick glue that holds stone or bricks together in modern houses. Instead, the Inka mastered the art of fitting stones together so that gravity alone locked them into place.

The walls of Inka terraces are strong enough that some even include floating staircases. Long stones stick out of walls to form steps. These floating steps do not look very sturdy, but they have survived centuries of use.

The Inka also built drainage into the terrace walls. When the soil behind the wall is very wet, some of the moisture can escape through the wall and continue down the hill.

The Inka were skillful builders. They built things with care so that they would last a long time.

The Inka used white stones to build this llama in a terrace wall in Peru.

This man uses a chakitaqlla.

TECHNOLOGY

Foot Power

Inka tools had to be lightweight and portable so they could be carried up and down terraces. Instead of using a heavy plow dragged behind an ox or a horse, the Inka used a *chakitaqlla* to break up hard ground before planting. Inka farmers drove these long, pointed sticks into the ground by pressing down on a bar with their feet. This simple tool is so well suited to the Andes that it is still used.

Inka floating staircase

Once a terrace wall was completed, people filled in the area behind the wall. What materials they used depended on what the terrace would be used for. Many terrace walls were used for agricultural reasons. Those types of terraces used similar materials. First, the Inka added rocks and gravel. Next, they added sand. Then, they added rich soil on top of the sand. Layers of rock, sand, and soil are **essential** to managing water. Each of these layers interacts with water differently.

Soil soaks up water. It expands slightly, almost like a sponge. Sand absorbs some water, but not as much as soil. Water flows quickly through the bottom layer of gravel and rocks. If terraces were filled with just soil, the stone wall would eventually break. The cycle of the soil expanding when wet and shrinking when dry would put too much stress on the wall. But Inka terraces are carefully designed so there's enough soil for plant roots but enough sand and rock to ensure proper drainage.

Archaeologists have discovered an unexpected benefit of terraces. During the day, stone walls soak up heat from the sun. At night, that heat slowly releases into the soil, protecting fragile plant roots from the cold. Terraces are also effective at **conserving** water by retaining moisture even in dry periods.

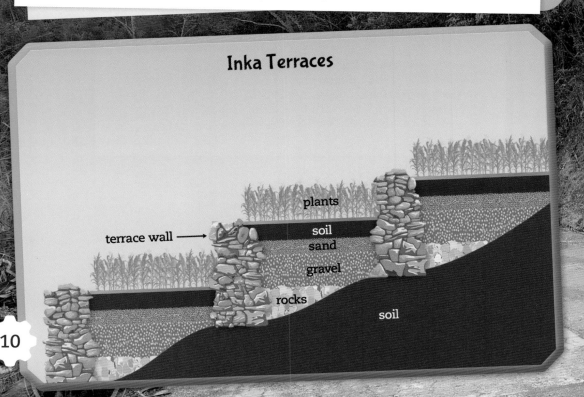

Inka Terraces

plants
soil
sand
gravel
rocks
soil
terrace wall →

These waterfalls were built into Inka terrace walls.

This wall of tires helps to control erosion.

Tiers of Tires

Terraces are still built in many areas. People have found that stacked tires can become a wall, while shredded tires can be substituted for gravel as part of a drainage system. Terraces are a great way to reuse tires instead of throwing them into landfills.

A terraced hill in the Andes can contain many different planting environments. For example, terraces toward the top of a hill are often colder. Terraces that are lower are warmer. Other hills might block sunlight from reaching certain areas, creating additional temperature differences. Some areas might be exposed to heavy winds. Other nearby areas might be protected from wind. Because of these differences, a crop might grow well in one spot and not grow at all just a few feet away.

For the Inka, this was not a problem. In fact, it was an advantage. Inka farmers planted many different crops in one terraced field. Potatoes, corn, and quinoa (KEEN-wah) were staples. Amazingly, about 4,000 potato varieties grow in the Andes.

Peruvian potatoes

The *huaña* (WAH-nyuh) potato is small and pink. It is very bitter, but it can be stored up to three years and grows even in a drought.

Farmers in the Andes today often experiment, testing to see where certain crops grow best. They sometimes grow hundreds of types of potatoes in a single field. Some types of potatoes are resistant to certain bugs. Some can survive frost. Others can grow even in a drought or a very wet year. By planting many types of crops, a farmer can be sure that at least some will grow.

Quinoa has become very popular around the world because of its unique taste and high protein content, which makes it a good substitute for meat.

Corn crops grow in Peru.

A Palace in the Clouds

Before 1911, only the people who lived nearby knew about the old stone ruins of Machu Picchu (MAH-choo PEE-choo). Then, a professor named Hiram Bingham came across the site. Some families lived nearby in wooden huts, farming small plots of land at the top of the mountain. A local man from the area led Bingham around the ruins.

Today, Machu Picchu is one of the most famous places in the world. It is believed that it was built to be a royal **estate**. It is perched high atop a steep mountain. It looks **precarious** but it has survived for centuries.

Water expert Kenneth R. Wright knows a lot about Inka building methods. He thinks that the Inka spent a year or two studying the site before they began to build. Once they started building, the Inka needed about 90 years to finish the **complex**.

After Bingham returned to the United States, he went into politics. He became a U.S. Senator in 1924.

14

Machu Picchu receives a huge amount of rain each year. Mudslides are a big threat. About 700 terraces fight against erosion. It is almost like the terraces pin down the mountain, holding it in place. The stonework at Machu Picchu rests on deep underground foundations. Wright thinks that the Inka builders spent about half their time working on just the foundations.

aftermath of a mudslide

Machu Picchu

When archaeologists studied a stone courtyard, they found out how far the Inka went to manage water. Just like when they built terraces, the Inka created good drainage by layering soil, sand, and rocks. At Machu Picchu, it happened on a huge scale.

For 1 meter (3 feet) under the stones of the courtyard, archaeologists found nothing but soil. Then, they came across sand and gravel. As they continued digging, they found granite chips. The granite was left from building Machu Picchu. Archaeologists had to dig about 3 m (9 ft.) before they got to the bottom of the drainage system!

Inka engineers designed for water in another way too. They created a canal system to bring water to the complex. The water was not for farming. It was for comfort and ease. The emperor and everyone else at Machu Picchu could get fresh water whenever they wanted.

High above the palace, a spring gurgles out of the ground. It collects in a pool. Then, it pours into a canal. The Inka made the canal from carefully cut stones. They sealed it with clay so that no water escaped between the stones.

The entire 760 m (2,500 ft.) canal runs slightly downhill. Gravity pushes the water toward its destination.

Inka canal

16

waterfalls from an Inka spring

SCIENCE

What Is a Spring?

When rain falls, water seeps into the ground. Eventually, this underground water pools into aquifers, which are like underground lakes. When an aquifer is full and water is forced to the surface, a spring results. Clean, naturally filtered water bursts from the ground.

two of Machu Picchu's
16 fountains

Average Rainfall in Peru

Month	Rain (mm)
Jan	154
Feb	119
Mar	109
Apr	41
May	9
Jun	18
Jul	8
Aug	10
Sep	14
Oct	47
Nov	77
Dec	110

The spring that feeds into the canal does not produce the same amount of water all year. Its flow depends on how much rain falls, how much snow melts, and other factors.

Inka engineers designed the canal so that it worked even when the spring's flow was weak. They also built two safety devices in case too much water rushed through the canal. The first spilled extra water into fields used for farming. The second spilled it into a drain in the city.

Once the water reached Machu Picchu, it flowed through a series of fountains. The first fountain was next to the emperor's door. He drank the freshest, cleanest water. From the emperor's fountain, the water went down a drain. It reappeared one level down in another fountain. The water went down another drain. It again reappeared another level down, pouring from a fountain. In all, Machu Picchu had 16 fountains. Everyone in the complex could easily get fresh water.

To make the fountains even more convenient, Inka builders made the flow of water the perfect width to fill an *arybalo*. This Inka jug has a narrow opening. The fountains directed the water into a tight, controlled arc.

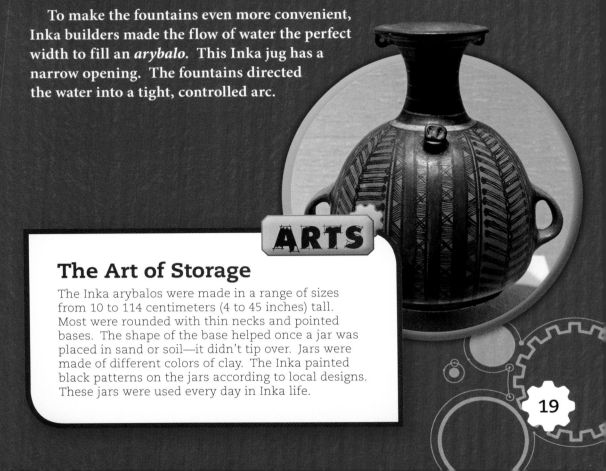

ARTS

The Art of Storage

The Inka arybalos were made in a range of sizes from 10 to 114 centimeters (4 to 45 inches) tall. Most were rounded with thin necks and pointed bases. The shape of the base helped once a jar was placed in sand or soil—it didn't tip over. Jars were made of different colors of clay. The Inka painted black patterns on the jars according to local designs. These jars were used every day in Inka life.

19

More Marvels

Tipón and Moray (moh-RAY) are not as famous as Machu Picchu, but they are both stunning. These sites demonstrate Inka water and land management.

Tipón was a royal estate. It is made up of 13 rectangular fields. They are supported by terraces. A canal brings water to nearby farming areas. It also brings water to the top two terraces. A spring supplies the other terraces with water.

Archaeologists have restored Tipón. The system of canals works as it did during the time of the Inka. The flow of water is dazzling and complex.

ruins of Tipón in Cusco Valley, Peru

One of the site's main fountains is a vivid example. Two canals merge together, then split into four channels. The four channels spill over a rock, creating a fountain. The water merges again. Then it divides yet again, going down separate channels. In all, Tipón's spring feeds three main canals. Each canal forks multiple times.

The way Tipón was built gave the Inka control over water. Stones can be inserted into the canals to cut off the flow of water. This results in more water flowing elsewhere. All the canals at Tipón work with both a heavy and a weak flow of water.

These four channels create

At Tipón, water drops up to 4.5 m (15 ft.) as it pours from one terrace to another. These drops presented Inka builders with a challenge. A big splash at the bottom would waste water and hurt the overall artistic effect of calm and control.

The solution was to create vertical channels—grooves built into the stone. The water does not spill over the wall like a waterfall. Instead, the channel keeps the water in a straight, controlled line. The splash when the water meets the ground is small and quiet.

Wright, the water expert, calls Tipón a "water garden." According to Wright, "the controlled rush of flowing and falling water" creates "**hydraulic** poetry." Wright and others believe that Tipón was a statement. By building it, the Inka displayed their dominance over water.

If Tipón is the peak of Inka water management, Moray might be the **pinnacle** of Inka terrace building. At Moray, terraces take the shape of circles. They don't climb up a hill or mountain. Instead, they fall into the earth.

No one knows why the Inka built Moray. One theory is that the site was for research. Inka scientists might have used Moray to study crops and create new **hybrids** of corn and other plants.

terrace walls at Moray

Drink Up

How much of the water at Tipón was used by people for washing, cooking, and drinking? How much was left for plants? Experts have tried to answer these questions. About 80 people lived at Tipón. If they each used 10 liters (2.6 gallons) of water per day, they used 800 L (211 gal.) per day total. The spring at Tipón produces about 1,000 L (264 gal.) of water per minute. People could use all the water they wanted—and barely make an impact!

The vertical channels on this fountain at Tipón help keep the splashes small.

23

Some people think Moray was built for other reasons. The terraces at Moray were made very carefully. They form almost perfect circles. This effort may mean the site was used for ceremonies of some kind.

Some people think Moray was a giant **amphitheater**. Moray has unusual **acoustics**. Voices are easy to hear, even from far away.

One thing that is clear is that people have been at Moray for a very long time. Some of the terraces date back before the Inka came to power, and people farmed at Moray up until the 1970s. Some farmers even remember which crops grew best at different locations.

the Inka site of Moray

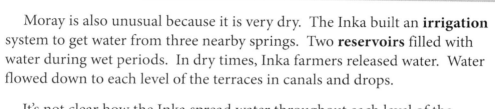

Moray is also unusual because it is very dry. The Inka built an **irrigation** system to get water from three nearby springs. Two **reservoirs** filled with water during wet periods. In dry times, Inka farmers released water. Water flowed down to each level of the terraces in canals and drops.

It's not clear how the Inka spread water throughout each level of the terraces. An underground irrigation system may have been used. If so, it has not yet been found. For now, Moray remains a beautiful mystery.

In the early 1930s, Moray was rediscovered by the outside world when people flying overhead saw the terraces.

Engineering Solutions for the Future

People in the Andes live in a challenging environment. The high mountains make travel difficult. Weather can be extreme. Even breathing can be hard due to a lack of oxygen in higher elevations.

People in the Andes face new challenges today. Erosion washes away good soil. Modern food can be cheap, but it is not always healthy. Because of climate change, weather is becoming drier. Temperature changes are becoming more extreme.

Some engineers are turning to the past for ideas. Organizations are helping farmers fix terraces and canals. Inka structures can be fixed by hand, without electric tools. Stone and clay are cheap or free. Building the Inka way does not require many shopping trips.

The Cusichaca Trust is restoring this area in Peru.

The Cusichaca Trust is one organization leading the effort to restore Inka terraces. Its goal is for everyone in Peru to have a secure source of food and water.

People are returning to the Inka technique of growing mixed crops together in the same field. The crops help and protect each other. Traditional crops, such as squash and quinoa, are also very healthy. Farmers are even rediscovering Inka crops that are rarely planted today, but that might grow well in a changing climate.

All over the former empire, Inka terraces are a clear reminder of the past. But the Inka people and their engineering ways are also part of the future.

A modern-day farmer harvests quinoa.

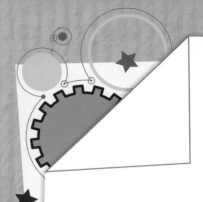

STEAM CHALLENGE

Define the Problem

Rainfall on mountain slopes moves downward and may cause mudslides and erosion. The Inka built terraces to decrease the force and to control the flow of water. Your task is to design and build a model of a layered terrace system that can hold 1 liter (about 1 quart) of water without spilling over the bottom terrace.

Constraints: Your model must include four terrace layers, and it must be able to hold 1 L (about 1 qt.) of water.

Criteria: A successful model will allow 1 L (about 1 qt.) of water to flow from the top to the bottom terrace layers. The water should not spill or overflow once it reaches the bottom terrace.

Research and Brainstorm

How did the Inka benefit from building terraces? What other techniques did Inka engineers use to manage water?

Design and Build

Sketch your terrace system. What purpose will each part serve? What materials will work best? Build the model.

Test and Improve

Pour 1 L (about 1 qt.) of water into the top of the system. Does the water flow in a controlled manner? Does your terrace system absorb all the water? Did it spill over once it reached the bottom layer? How can you improve it? Modify your design and try again.

Reflect and Share

What other materials can you use to build the model? Can you add more layers to your design? How can you modify your design to make water move more quickly or more slowly through the system?

Glossary

acoustics—the qualities of a place that affect how sound travels in it

amphitheater—an outdoor arena for music, plays, or other events

archaeologists—people who study things that cultures leave behind

canals—systems of outdoor pipes, streams, or rivers made by people to deliver or connect water

complex—a group of buildings that are near each other and are used for particular purposes

conserving—saving or using less

debris—pieces left behind after something has been damaged or destroyed

drought—a long period of time in which there is little to no rain

erosion—the gradual destruction of something by natural forces

essential—necessary and extremely important

estate—a large house surrounded by other buildings

fertile—able to support the growth of many crops or plants

hybrids—new plants created by crossing two different species of plants

hydraulic—brought about by means of water

irrigation—a system of bringing water to an area for plants

pinnacle—the highest point

precarious—not safe, strong, or steady

reservoirs—artificial lakes or other bodies of water created to store water

resistant—not harmed or affected by something

vineyards—places where grapes for wine are grown

Index

Do you want to learn how cultures design solutions for problems?
Here are some tips to get you started.

"I've always loved languages and learning about other cultures. I had lots of pen pals from other countries when I was in school. Ask your friends and family what problems they have. Then, design interesting solutions for those problems!" —*Amy Van Allen, Senior Project Manager*

"As a writer and editor in a museum, I combine my own Native American culture with a love of sharing stories. It is important to know how your culture designs solutions. Then, join the school newspaper, yearbook club, or write your thoughts in a journal to share your stories." —*Tanya Thrasher (Cherokee Nation), Publications Manager and Editor-In-Chief*